THE WICKED WIT OF
WINSTON
CHURCHILL

THE WICKED WIT OF
WINSTON
CHURCHILL

Compiled, edited and introduced by

Dominique Enright

Michael O'Mara Books Limited

This revised edition
first published in Great Britain in 2011 by
Michael O'Mara Books Limited
9 Lion Yard
Tremadoc Road
London SW4 7NQ

A CIP catalogue record for this book
is available from the British Library.

Papers used by Michael O'Mara Books Limited are natural, recyclable
products made from wood grown in sustainable forests.
The manufacturing processes conform to the environmental
regulations of the country of origin.

ISBN: 978-1-84317-565-0

7 9 10 8

www.mombooks.com

Designed and typeset by Design 23

Printed and bound by CPI Group (UK) Ltd, Croydon, CR0 4YY

Contents

'It is a good thing for an
uneducated man to read books
of quotations.'
My Early Life, 1930

Introduction

Sir Winston Leonard Spencer Churchill was born in 1874 at Blenheim Palace, Oxfordshire, the eldest son of Lord Randolph Churchill and his American wife, and a nephew of the Duke of Marlborough. Despite an undistinguished career at Harrow, he attended the RMA, Sandhurst, before being gazetted to the 4th Hussars. Following service in India and on the North-West Frontier, he took part in the Nile Expeditionary Force in the Sudan in 1898, and was attached to the 21st Lancers when that regiment made its famous mounted charge against the dervishes during the Battle of Omdurman. As a newspaper correspondent during the Boer War of 1899–1901 he was captured when the armoured train he was travelling in was ambushed and derailed, but later successfully escaped his captors and made an epic journey back to British lines. He was present at a number of the most famous battles of the campaign, including Spion Kop.

Churchill entered Parliament as a Conservative MP in 1900 but, finding himself increasingly at odds with the party, in 1906 crossed the floor of the House and joined the Liberal Party, becoming Under-Secretary for the Colonies in 1908 and President of the Board of Trade a year later, in which post he introduced labour exchanges. Appointed Home Secretary in 1910, he was involved in the Siege of Sidney

Street the following year, and not long afterwards changed his post for that of First Lord of the Admiralty, and thereafter worked furiously to prepare the Royal Navy for the war with Germany that he knew must come; he also worked tirelessly on the development and deployment of tanks, an invention for which (as was later officially acknowledged) he was partly responsible. In 1915 he resigned in the face of blame for the costly failure of the Dardanelles and Gallipoli operations, and went to France to take command of an infantry battalion on the Western Front. He returned to Britain in 1917 and took up the post of Minister of Munitions in the Coalition government now headed by Lloyd George. He was Secretary for War and Air from 1919 to 1921, but in 1924 changed allegiance once more when he was elected to a different constituency as a 'constitutionalist' Conservative; from then until 1929 he served as Chancellor of the Exchequer.

Without office in the 1930s under Ramsay MacDonald's National government and the succeeding Tory administrations, he increasingly warned from the backbenches of the dangers of German rearmament, of appeasement of the dictators, and of Britain's absolute lack of preparedness for war, referring to the Munich settlement of 1938 as 'a total and unmitigated defeat'. The fall of Norway in May 1940, and the imminent threat to British forces in France and to Britain herself, led to a vote of no confidence in the administration headed by Neville Chamberlain, whom Churchill succeeded as Prime Minister, immediately forming a Coalition government.

Introduction

Despite the disasters in Belgium and France, victory in the Battle of Britain, followed by successes at sea and in North Africa, helped to stiffen the country's sinews, aided immeasurably by Churchill's leadership and his oratory. His close personal friendship with President Roosevelt ensured American support and, following Japanese and German declarations of war against the USA in December 1941, did much to smooth the often rocky path of inter-Allied co-operation, while his ability both to flatter and to stand up to Stalin promoted a relationship with the Soviet Union that helped to ensure the defeat of the Axis. After German defeats in North Africa and Russia, and American naval victories over the Japanese in the Pacific, the tide of war began to turn, and Churchill increasingly directed his formidable talents to the total defeat of Germany, Italy and Japan and the maintenance of the Triple Alliance which was to bring that about. He was not to share in the final triumph, however; in the general election of July 1945, two months after Germany's unconditional surrender, the war-weary British people voted the Labour Party into power, and Churchill handed over the premiership to Clement Attlee.

He remained an untiring leader of the Opposition, while his fame and reputation ensured that he maintained an overwhelming presence on the international stage. In 1951, aged seventy-seven, he became Prime Minister again, resigning in 1955 in favour of the much younger Anthony Eden, although he stayed on as a backbencher well into his old age, until failing health forced him to give up his seat in Parliament. He died, full of years and honours, in 1965 and, after a magnificent state funeral, was buried in the graveyard of the tiny parish church close to Blenheim Palace, the house in which he had been born.

'The characteristic of a great man is his power to leave a lasting impression on people he meets,' Churchill once said. Was he thinking of himself? He was certainly not blind to his own stature. He was one of the few people who can truly be said to have been larger than life. His life was not only long but it was full and varied – full of friends, and of enemies; full of action and creativity, of argument and ruthlessness. There were many who loved him, many who hated him, and many, it seems, who both loved and hated him. Exuberant and spoiled, childish and childlike, kind and cruel, enquiring but pig-headed, hardworking and generous but conceited and determined to be centre-stage . . . Churchill was all of these things. Remembered as a political leader, as a wartime strategist, and as the last of the great public orators, Churchill's fame also rests upon his many books, notably his histories. These include *The World Crisis* (four volumes, 1923–9), *Marlborough* (four volumes, 1933–8), *The Second World War* (six volumes, 1948–54) and *A History of the English-Speaking*

Peoples (four volumes, 1956–8), besides numerous volumes of speeches and broadcasts, volumes of autobiography, a biography of his father, one rather poor novel, *Savrola* ('I have consistently urged my friends to abstain from reading it.'), and countless articles, including some on painting which were published as a book, *Painting as a Pastime*. Altogether he published more words than Charles Dickens and Walter Scott together – 'more books than Moses', he once joked.

He painted well enough for the painter Sir John Lavery to say: 'Had he chosen painting instead of statesmanship I believe he would have been a great master with the brush', and his work, under the name Charles Morin, was accepted by the Louvre. He had the inventive imagination and mental application to devise the tank: '. . . fit up a number of steam tractors with small armoured shelters, in which men and machine-guns could be placed, which would be bullet-proof . . . The caterpillar system would enable trenches to be crossed quite easily, and the weight of the machine would destroy all wire entanglements,' he wrote to the Prime Minister, Herbert Asquith, in January 1915. In addition, he played polo, was a fine shot – and enjoyed bricklaying, even accepting an invitation to join the Amalgamated Union of Building Trade Workers. For someone whose formal education was less than full, this list of achievements is especially impressive. However it may be, Churchill himself suggested that his slow progress at school might have been a hidden blessing: 'By being so long in the lowest form I gained an immense advantage over the cleverer boys . . . I got into my bones the essential structure of the normal British sentence – which is a noble thing.'

'He mobilized the English language and sent it into battle,' said John F. Kennedy in 1963 when granting Churchill US citizenship. There are those who believe that during the Second World War it was the inspiring power of his speeches that kept up morale and ultimately led the Allies to victory. Others were less enchanted: 'In private conversation,' complained the writer and administrator Lionel Curtis, 'he tries on speeches like a man trying on ties in his bedroom to see how he would look in them.' Of the orator and his audience, Churchill said:

Before he can inspire them with any emotion, he must be swayed by it himself. When he would rouse their indignation, his heart is filled with anger. Before he can move their tears, his own must flow. To convince them, he must himself believe. His opinions may change as their impressions fade, but every orator means what he says at the moment he says it. He is never consciously insincere.

Asked by Adlai Stevenson, in 1955, on what he based his oratorical style, Churchill told him: 'America – and Bourke Cockran, who taught me to use every note of the human voice as if playing an organ.' Churchill had met Cockran, a New York politician, on his first visit to the United States sixty years before, and they remained friends over the years. Cockran, said Churchill, 'could play on every emotion and hold thousands of people riveted . . . when he spoke'. Yet it is Churchill who is remembered for his oratory. It might be because Churchill was a very emotional man himself – and not ashamed of showing his feelings ('I blub an awful lot, you know. You'll have to get used to it,' he warned Anthony Montague Browne soon after the latter's appointment as his Private Secretary) – that he could strike a chord in the emotions of his listeners. Which is not to say that he did not also manipulate his words: 'There is no finer investment for any community than putting milk into babies,' he said in a 1943 radio broadcast – he had a fine ear for the heartstring-tugging phrase and the chorus of 'Aahs' can almost be heard. This was also, however, an aspect of his soft-heartedness – which could on occasion descend to the absurd, as when this ruthless politician – who had called upon the nation to fight, fight, fight, and never surrender – while watching a film of *Oliver Twist* at home put a hand over his dog Rufus's eyes so that Rufus would not see Bill Sikes attempt to drown his dog. Or as when he would hand a book to his secretary saying to 'put it away, Toby has read it' – Toby being his budgerigar who, along with a cat, had the run of his bedroom (and of his guests – Jock Colville, one of Churchill's Private Secretaries, relates counting fourteen budgie droppings on Rab Butler's bald head one day when, as Chancellor of the Exchequer, Butler had spent some time at Churchill's bedside going through budget papers with the Prime Minister, who liked to work in bed. Butler himself told of an earlier such visit to Chequers, in 1943 – he had found the Prime Minister in bed, with Nelson the cat curled up on his feet: 'This cat', declared Churchill, 'does more for the war effort than you do. He acts as a hotwater bottle and saves fuel and power.'

Churchill's ability with words was not only employed in sonorous speeches (most of which were fine oratory but not wicked wit), but also in his impish – indeed, often childish – sense of humour.

He could not resist making a quip – occasionally even when he did not actually mean what he was saying – to the extent that over the years many witty remarks whose provenance is in fact far from certain have been ascribed to him. Some he denied – but might well have been responsible for; others that he was not responsible for he might well have been quite happy to have credited to him. Thus of those witticisms and stories that follow not every single one can be guaranteed to have originated with Churchill – but they could have, and some he would have liked to have coined. Whistler's comment to Oscar Wilde when the playwright remarked, 'How I wish I had said that' comes to mind: 'You will, Oscar, you will.'

DOMINIQUE ENRIGHT

Timeline of Winston Churchill's Life

1874 born 30 November in Blenheim Palace, Woodstock, Oxfordshire, to Lord Randolph Churchill, a politician who served as Chancellor of the Exchequer, and Jenny Jerome, an American socialite

1879–88 attends school at St George's School in Ascot, Berkshire, followed by Brunswick School in Hove

1888 moves to Harrow School in April, where he starts his military career, joining the Harrow Rifle Corps upon his arrival

1893–4 Churchill enters Sandhurst Royal Military College on 1 September, graduating in December the following year

1895 receives his first commission as a Second Lieutenant on 20 February in the 4th Queen's Own Hussars. He travels to Cuba to observe the Spanish fight the Cuban guerrillas

1896–7 is promoted to Lieutenant and travels to India with his regiment. Sees action on the North-West Frontier. Also writes for *The Pioneer* and *The Daily Telegraph*

1898 is transferred to Egypt and joins the 21st Lancers, serving in the Sudan

1899 resigns from the British Army in May. First foray into politics, running and losing the by-election as the Conservative candidate for Oldham

1899 obtains commission to act as war correspondent for the *Morning Post* on the outbreak of the Second Boer War. He is captured and imprisoned while on a scouting mission, escaping a few weeks later. Churchill then rejoins the army on its march to relieve the British at the Siege of Ladysmith

1900 Churchill retires from the army and again stands for Parliament in the general election, winning the Oldham seat for the Conservatives

1902 joins the Imperial Yeomanry where he is commissioned as Captain in the Queen's Own Oxfordshire Hussars

1904 changes allegiance from the Conservatives to the Liberal party after opposition to Joseph Chamberlain's trade tariffs

1905 as a Liberal, Churchill becomes Under-Secretary for State for the Colonies. He is also promoted to Major in the Hussars

1906 becomes MP for Manchester North West in the general election (1906-8). Publishes *Lord Randolph Churchill* and *My African Journey*

1908 promoted to the Cabinet as President of the Board of Trade. Becomes MP for Dundee (1908-12)

1908 marries Clementine Hozier on 12 September

1909 Diana, the first of his five children, born on 11 July.

1910-11 promoted to Home Secretary

1911-15 becomes First Lord of the Admiralty. Supports development of naval aviation and tanks, and construction of newer and larger warships

1915 as one of the architects of the disastrous Gallipoli landings, he takes much of the blame, and is demoted in Asquith's all-party coalition

1915–6 spends time on the Western Front. Appointed Lieutenant-Colonel of the 6th Battalion Royal Scots fusiliers

1917 appointed Minister of Munitions

1919 Churchill becomes Secretary of State for War and Air. Staunch advocate of foreign intervention while in the War Office, hoping to strangle Bolshevism while it was still in its infancy

1921 becomes Secretary of State for the Colonies, and is a signatory of the Anglo-Irish Treaty, establishing the Irish Free State

1922 loses his seat as MP for Dundee in the general election

1924 becomes MP for Epping in the general election (1924-45). Rejoins the Conservative Party, and is appointed Chancellor of the Exchequer under Stanley Baldwin

1929 Conservative government is defeated in general election, beginning Churchill's 'Wilderness Years'

1930–9 spends much of his time campaigning against Indian independence and warning of the threat of fascism and Germany's rearmament. Publishes *My Early Life, Thoughts and Adventures, Marlborough: His Life and Times, Great Contemporaries* and *Step by Step*

1939 on 3 September Britain declares war on Germany. Churchill is appointed First Lord of the Admiralty and member of the War Cabinet once again; the Fleet simply informed: 'Winston is back'

1940 on 10 May Chamberlain resigns as Prime Minister. Churchill is supported as his replacement. Refuses to consider an armistice with Germany, his use of rhetoric hardening public opinion

1941 the Soviet Union enters the war after Germany invades. The Japanese attack Pearl Harbor. Britain declares war on Japan. Germany and Italy declare war on the USA

1942 Churchill approves the policy of saturation bombing of German cities

1943 the Allies drive Germany out of North Africa and invade Sicily and mainland Italy

1944 6 June: D-Day

1945 Victory in Europe. Churchill's government is defeated in the general election. Japan surrenders after two nuclear bombs devastate Hiroshima and Nagasaki

1946 gives his 'Iron Curtain' speech in Missouri

1951 re-elected as Prime Minister

1955 resigns after a series of strokes start to limit him mentally and physically

1964 stands down at the general election

1965 dies after a severe stroke on 24 January, aged ninety

Be killed
many times:
Politics

The political arena is famously a battleground where the weapons are words, and many are the insults that flow back and forth across the parliamentary floor.

'The world today is ruled by harassed politicians absorbed in getting into office or turning out the other man so that not much room is left for debating great issues on their merits.'

'Politics are almost as exciting as war, and quite as dangerous. In war you can only be killed once, but in politics many times.'

On the qualities required by a politician:
'The ability to foretell what is going to happen tomorrow, next week, next month, and next year.
And to have the ability afterwards to explain why it didn't happen.'

'I always avoid prophesying beforehand, because it is much better policy to prophesy after the event has already taken place.'

'Balfour is wicked and moral. Asquith is good and immoral.'

'When I was called upon to be Prime Minister, now nearly two years ago, there were not many applicants for the job. Since then perhaps the market has improved.'

To an MP who repeatedly interrupted one of his speeches: 'The honourable gentleman should really not generate more indignation that he can conveniently contain.'

'No one pretends that democracy is perfect or allwise. Indeed, it has been said that democracy is the worst form of Government except all those other forms that have been tried from time to time.'

'The high belief in the perfection of man is appropriate in a man of the cloth but not in a prime minister.'

WSC's definition of a parliamentary candidate:
'He is asked to stand, he wants to sit, he is expected to lie.'

On the difference between a candidate and an MP:
'One stands for a place – the other sits for it.'

'The Conservative Party is not a party but a conspiracy.'

'Tory democracy is a democracy which supports the Tories.'

'The Tory fault – a yearning for mediocrity.'

'Reconstructing a Cabinet is like solving a kaleidoscopic jigsaw puzzle.'

'Headmasters have powers at their disposal with which Prime Ministers have never been invested.'

WSC: We have all heard how Dr Guillotine was executed
by the instrument he invented –
Sir Herbert Samuel: He was not.
WSC: Well, he ought to have been.

'It would be a great reform in politics if wisdom could be made to spread as easily and as rapidly as folly.'

Of the Labour Party in 1945:
'They are not fit to manage a whelk stall.'

On being interrupted by a political rival:
'I do not challenge the honourable gentleman when the truth leaks out of him from time to time.'

Of WSC's (then) fellow Conservatives:
'They are a class of right honourable gentlemen – all good men, all honest men – who are ready to make great sacrifices for their opinions, but they have no opinions. They are ready to die for the truth, if only they knew what the truth was.'

'Some men change their party for the sake of their principles; others change their principles for the sake of their party.'

On a fellow Liberal MP joining the Socialist Party:
'It is the only time I've ever seen a rat swimming towards a sinking ship.'

'To improve is to change; to be perfect is to change often.'

'I see it is said that leaders should keep their ears to the ground. All I can say is that the British nation will find it very hard to look up to the leaders who are detected in that somewhat ungainly posture.'

'When I am abroad, I always make it a rule never to criticize or attack the government of my own country. I make up for lost time when I get home.'

According to legend, during the late 1920s or early 1930s, at a time when Churchill was speaking out against those who argued that the League of Nations and the power of civilized negotiation would secure peace, and calling for greater expenditure on defence, he addressed the St George Society. His theme was how a contemporary St George would save a maiden from the dragon.

'St George would be accompanied, not by a horse, but by a delegation. He would be armed not with a lance, but by a secretariat . . . he would propose a conference with the dragon – a Round Table conference – no doubt that would be more convenient for the dragon's tail.

'Then after making a trade agreement with the dragon, St George would lend the dragon a lot of money.' He continued in this vein for a bit, until 'The maiden's release would be referred to the League of Nations of Geneva, and finally St George would be photographed with the dragon.'

'The inherent vice of capitalism is the unequal sharing of blessings; the inherent virtue of socialism is the equal sharing of miseries.'

'There is not one single social or economic principle or concept in the philosophy of the Russian Bolshevik which has not been realized, carried into action, and enshrined in immutable laws a million years ago by the white ant.'

'Trying to maintain good relations with a Communist is like wooing a crocodile. You do not know whether to tickle it under the chin or beat it over the head. When it opens its mouth, you cannot tell whether it is trying to smile or preparing to eat you up.'

'Politics is like waking up in the morning. You never know whose head you'll find on the pillow.'

*On being repeatedly interrupted during a
speech to the Commons:*
'The honourable gentleman . . . has arrogated to himself a
function which did not belong to him, namely to make my
speech instead of letting me make it.'

S ome time after he ceded the premiership to Eden,
Churchill was sitting in an armchair in the Members' Bar
of the House of Commons. He was alone. Three young Tory
MPs entered and, failing to see the old boy slouched in his
armchair, began to chatter loudly. It soon became clear that
the Member for Epping was the subject of their talk.

'You know,' one remarked, 'it's very sad about old Winston.
He's getting awfully forgetful.'

'Shame, isn't it?' said another. 'He's really very doddery
now, I gather.'

'Not only that,' added the third, 'but I've heard that he's
going a bit – *you* know – *ga-ga*.'

'Yesh,' rumbled a deep voice from the nearby armchair,
'an' they shay he'sh gettin' terribly deaf, as well!'

Terminological Diversions:
Words

Churchill's love of words revealed itself above all in the way he enjoyed playing with them. On one occasion it ensured that he lost a game of golf. Violet Bonham-Carter described a round of golf he was playing against her father, the Prime Minister Herbert Asquith. Churchill, who could play a good game when not diverted – but was easily diverted – was well ahead of Asquith until he spotted a shrub with orange berries. Violet Asquith, as she then was, told him it was buckthorn, 'the olive of the north'. 'He rose', she wrote, 'like a trout to the fly of any phrase and his attention was immediately arrested and deflected from the game. "The olive of the north – that's good. The buckthorn of the south – that's not so good" and during the remaining holes he rang the changes on every possible combination and permutation of this meagre theme, which took his mind and eye completely off the ball.' To Asquith's delight Churchill didn't hit another ball that afternoon and lost the game.

On receiving another honorary degree:
'Perhaps no one has ever passed so few examinations and received so many degrees.'

'Men will forgive a man anything except bad prose.'

'This is the sort of English up with which I will not put.'

'We must have a better word than "prefabricated".
Why not "ready-made"?'

Referring to the Government's denial of the exploitation of Chinese coolies in South Africa:
'Perhaps we have been guilty of some terminological inexactitudes.'

Surveying the destroyers sent to Britain by the USA under the Lend-Lease Agreement set up in 1940, Churchill gazed at the barely seaworthy vessels and mumbled to himself gloomily, 'Cheap and nasty.' 'Pardon me?' asked Roosevelt's envoy, standing next to him. Quick-thinking, the Prime Minister amended his remark: 'Cheap for us, and nasty for the Germans.'

'I do not think any expression of scorn or severity which I have heard used by our critics has come anywhere near the language I have been myself accustomed to use, not only orally, but in a stream of written minutes. In fact, I wonder that a great many of my colleagues are on speaking terms with me.'

On Sir Alfred Bossom, a member of the Conservative Party:
'Bossom? What an extraordinary name. Neither one thing nor the other!'

By 1953, Churchill was becoming somewhat deaf. The Italian government, as is still its wont, had just fallen, and the ousted Italian premier, a friend of WSC's told him, was planning to retire and read the works of Anthony Trollope.

There was a long silence. Then: 'Tell me more about that trollop,' said Churchill.

A few years later, an MP called Bernard Brain was speaking during a debate in the House of Commons. WSC couldn't see him and asked his neighbour, Julian Amery, a Conservative MP and son of WSC's old friend Leo Amery, who it was speaking. 'Braine,' answered Amery. 'James?' 'No, *Braine*.' 'Drain?' said Churchill. 'He can't be called Drain. Nobody's called Drain.'

Finding a scrap of paper, Julian Amery wrote the name down. 'Ah, I see,' Churchill said. '. . . Is he well named?'

'The essential structure of the ordinary British sentence . . . is a noble thing.'

On the use of the passive:
'What if I had said, instead of "We shall fight on the beaches", "Hostilities will be engaged with our adversary on the coastal perimeter"?'

'*The Times* is speechless and takes three columns to express its speechlessness.'

'I think "No comment" is a splendid expression. I am using it again and again. I got it from Sumner Welles [the American diplomat and writer].'

In a memo to the Admiralty after repeated reports of British shipping losses:
'Must we have this lugubrious ingemination of the news of our shipping losses?'

On a tour of Africa in 1907: '
So fari – go goodi!'

'Short words are best and the old words when short
are best of all.'

> *On a Member's statement that economic planning
> was baloney:*
> 'I should prefer to have an agreed definition of
> the meaning of "baloney" before I attempt to
> deal with such a topic.'

There is a story that on a parliamentary paper that was being circulated, someone scribbled in the margin against a statement with which he disagreed the words 'Round objects!' He was probably congratulating himself on his wit, and thinking how the PM would appreciate his droll comment, when the paper made its way back to him – beside his words was scrawled in Churchill's handwriting: 'Who is Round? And why does he object?'

'Pigs treat us as equals': Animals, Real and Metaphorical

Although Winston Churchill is, rightly, famed as an orator and his speeches noted for the rolling fluidity of their language and their power to move and inspire, most of them could not be described as wicked or witty, except in so far as there is a kind of wit in the way he uses language – in the metaphors he employs. Interestingly, animals often figure – as allusions but most often as metaphors in his speeches. Churchill liked animals; sometimes he found this difficult to reconcile with his fondness for rich food. Anthony Montague Brown recalled that 'One Christmas he was about to carve a goose. Learning it was one of his own, he put down the knife and fork and said, "I could not possibly eat a bird that I have known socially."'

'Dogs look up to men, cats look down on them, but pigs just treat us as equals.' He kept all of these animals – and others – but perhaps he felt a special affinity with pigs (charming and intelligent creatures that are much maligned): one of his Private Secretaries described being summoned to Churchill's bedroom where the Prime Minister was lying in bed looking like 'a rather nice pig in a silk suit'. Clementine's pet name for him was 'Pig'. (And apparently the KGB's wartime codename for Churchill was 'Boar' . . . not exactly unbreakable.) In Britain, during the war, however, he was depicted as a bulldog – seen as the 'British Bulldog', epitomizing the never-let-go, never-give-in spirit of the nation.

With his liking for words including the silliest of puns, Churchill called the henhouse he had built for his chickens 'Chickenham Palace'. (Perhaps he was thinking of its residents when he exclaimed 'Some chicken! Some neck!' – words quoted elsewhere in this book.)

'I could not possibly eat a bird that I have known socially.'

'Dogs look up to men, cats look down on them, but pigs just treat us as equals.'

'Although it may be very difficult to define in law what is or what is not a trade union, most people of common sense know a trade union when they see one. It is like trying to define a rhinoceros: it is difficult enough, but if one is seen, everybody can recognize it.'

WSC's name for the henhouse he built for his chickens: 'Chickenham Palace'

On Mussolini:

'The whipped jackal, who, to save his own skin, has made of Italy a vassal state of Hitler's Empire, is frisking up by the side of the German tiger with yelps not only of appetite – that could be understood – but even of triumph.'

On his appointment as First Lord of the Admiralty:
'This is because I can now lay eggs instead of scratching around in the dust and clucking. It is a far more satisfactory occupation. I am at present in process of laying a great number of eggs – "good eggs" every one of them. And there will be many more clutches to follow . . . New appointments to be made. Admirals to be "poached", "scrambled" and "buttered". A fresh egg from a fruitful hen.'

'Dictators ride to and fro upon tigers which they dare not dismount. And the tigers are getting hungry.'

'It was the nation and the race dwelling all round the globe that had the lion's heart. I had the luck to be called upon to give the roar. I also hope that I sometimes suggested to the lion the right place to use his claws.'

On being advised his fly buttons were undone: 'Dead birds don't fall out of their nests.'

To the French in October 1940: 'We are waiting for the long-promised invasion. So are the fishes.'

'Just as eels are supposed to get used to skinning, so politicians get used to being caricatured . . . If we must confess it, they are quite offended and downcast when the cartoons stop.'

'We are all worms. But I do believe that I am a glow-worm.'

In the Great Hall of Chequers is a large Rubens painting of the Aesop fable in which a lion caught in a net is rescued by a mouse nibbling at the rope binding the net to a tree. According to Harold Wilson, Churchill decided late one night: 'Can't see the moushe', and called for his paints and brushes. He then set about painting in the mouse.

Whatever the truth, some time later the painting was lent to a fund-raising exhibition for Churchill College, Cambridge, and was cleaned – if mouse there had been, it came off.

'Pigs treat us as equals'

'An appeaser is one who feeds a crocodile — hoping that it will eat him last.'

'We hoped to land a wildcat that would tear out the bowels of the Boche. Instead we have stranded a vast whale with its tail flopping about in the water!'

Making speeches, WSC is said to have claimed, is 'The art of making deep sounds from the stomach sound like important messages from the brain.' It is a great deal more than this, of course, as Churchill well knew. His friend Lord Birkenhead's quip, 'Winston has devoted the best years of his life to preparing his impromptu speeches', carries more than a grain of truth. Unlike many, if not most, statesmen, Churchill did not employ a speechwriter – he worked hard preparing his speeches, usually in bed, often remarking of those that were taking a lot of effort, 'This speech is hanging over me like a vulture.' He would also sometimes say, 'I'm going to make a long speech because I've not had the time to prepare a short one,' which is not as illogical as it sounds, as anyone who has had to condense an argument into a limited number of words will recognize. He also said of verbosity, 'It is sheer laziness not compressing thought into a reasonable space'.

On speechmaking:
'The art of making deep sounds from the stomach sound like important messages from the brain.'

'This speech is hanging over me like a vulture.'

'I'm going to make a long speech because I've not had the time to prepare a short one.'

On verbosity:
'It is sheer laziness not compressing thought into a reasonable space.'

'Call that a maiden speech? I call it a brazen hussy of a speech.'

Casting pearls

It is said that on one occasion during the war Churchill, due to deliver an address to the nation at eight p.m., for some reason had to take a taxi to the BBC studio. As one drew up, WSC's aide told the driver the destination. 'Sorry, guv, can't take you there, I've got to get home quick to listen to the Prime Minister's speech on me radio.'

This, of course, greatly pleased Churchill, who handed a five-pound note to his aide to pass on to the cabbie, saying, 'I'm in a hurry to get to that address.'

Delighted with the five pounds (a lot of money in those days), and hopeful of more to come, the cabbie quickly opened the passenger doors: 'Get in, guv'nor. Frig the bloody Prime Minister – what's that address again?'

When asked by a young MP how he could have put more fire into the speech he had just made:
'What you should have done is put the speech into the fire.'

On MP Lord Charles Beresford:
'He is one of those orators of whom it was well said, "Before they get up, they do not know what they are going to say; when they are speaking, they do not know what they are saying; and when they have sat down, they do not know what they have said." '
'I can well understand the Honourable Member's wishing to speak on. He needs the practice badly.'

'It may be an honour, but never a pleasure. There are only a few things from which I derive intense pleasure, and speaking is not one of them.'

'Let us not shrink from using the short expressive phrase even if it is conversational.'

'When I warned them [the French] that Britain would fight on alone whatever they did, their generals told their Prime Minister and his divided Cabinet: "In three weeks England will have her neck wrung like a chicken." Some chicken! Some neck!'

'Of course it is perfectly possible for honourable members to prevent my speaking, and indeed I do not want to cast my pearls before . . . those who do not want them.'

Friends
like these . . .

'I hate nobody except Hitler – and that is professional.' If one were to judge by the following, however, one would suppose Churchill, his fellow politicians and the military leaders were the bitterest of enemies. Some, it is true, he liked, and they liked him, whatever their politics. Others – such as the Welsh Labour MP Aneurin Bevan – he did not like. Whether or not they liked one another, however, was no obstacle to the insults they threw at each other.

On Field Marshal Lord Alanbrooke:
'When I thump the table and push my face towards him, what does he do? Thumps the table harder and glares back at me.'

On the Duke of Windsor:
'A little man dressed up to the nines.'

On Lord Macaulay:
'It is beyond our hopes to overtake Lord Macaulay ... We can only hope that Truth will follow swiftly enough to fasten the label "Liar" to his genteel coattails.'

Friends like these . . .

On Austen Chamberlain:
'He always played the game and he always lost it.'

On Arthur Balfour
(Conservative politician, and Prime Minister 1902–6):
'If you wanted nothing done, Arthur Balfour was the best
man for the task. There was no equal to him.'

'He would very soon have put Socrates in his place, if that
old fellow had played any of his dialectical tricks on him.
When I go to Heaven, I shall try to arrange a chat between
these two on some topic not too recondite for me to
follow.'

'The dignity of a prime minister, like a lady's virtue, is not
susceptible of partial diminution.'

On Joseph Chamberlain:
'Mr Chamberlain loves the working man; he loves to see him work.'

'The country thought Mr Chamberlain . . . was a prophet with a message. They found him a politician groping for a platform.'

On Lord Esher
(Reginald Baliol Brett, 2nd Viscount Esher,
government official, courtier and diarist,
and Liberal MP):

'We must conclude that an uncontrollable fondness for fiction forbade him to forsake it for fact. Such constancy is a defect in an historian.'

Friends like these . . .

On Stanley Baldwin:
'The Government cannot make up their minds, or they
cannot get the Prime Minister to make up his mind.
So they go on, in strange paradox, decided only to be
undecided, resolved to be irresolute, adamant for drift, solid
for fluidity, all powerful to be impotent.'

'I wish Stanley Baldwin no ill, but it would have been
much better if he had never lived.'

'In those days Mr Baldwin was wiser than he is now;
he used frequently to take my advice.'

'He has his ear so close to the ground that he has
locusts in it.'

'It is a fine thing to be honest, but it is also very important
to be right.'

'He occasionally stumbled over the truth, but hastily picked
himself up and hurried on as if nothing had happened.'

On Ramsay MacDonald
(Britain's first Labour Prime Minister):
'I remember, when I was a child, being taken to the celebrated Barnum's Circus, which contained an exhibition of freaks and monstrosities, but the exhibition on the programme which I most desired to see was one described as the "Boneless Wonder". My parents judged that spectacle would be too revolting and demoralizing for my young eyes, and I have waited fifty years to see the "Boneless Wonder" on thc Treasury Bench.'

'The greatest living master of falling without hurting himself.'

'We know that he has, more than any other man, the gift of compressing the largest amount of words into the smallest amount of thought.'

On Neville Chamberlain:
'An old town clerk looking at European affairs through the wrong end of a municipal drainpipe.'

'He has a lust for peace.'

'You were given the choice between war and dishonour. You chose dishonour and you will have war.'

'In the depths of that dusty soul there is nothing but abject surrender.'

'The only guide to a man is his conscience; the only shield to his memory is the rectitude and sincerity of his actions.'

On Field Marshal Sir Bernard Montgomery
(1st Viscount Montgomery of Alamein, one of Britain's most
successful military leaders):
'In defeat, unbeatable; in victory, unbearable.'

Anthony Montague Browne in his account of his years as Churchill's Private Secretary wrote of how much Churchill disliked being interrupted while he was at work. On one occasion in the 1950s, as he worked on a speech in bed, the Foreign Secretary and the Chancellor of the Exchequer (Eden and Butler) arrived to see him urgently. They followed his secretary upstairs and stood outside the bedroom door while Montague Browne went in to announce their visit to the Prime Minister. 'Tell them to go and bugger themselves,' they heard. Then, as Montague Browne was coming out: 'There is no need for them to carry out that instruction literally.'

On R. A. (Rab) Butler
(Conservative politician, who held important government positions,
including that of Chancellor):
'I am amused by the Chancellor of the Exchequer. He is
always patting himself on the back, a kind of exercise that
contributes to his excellent physical condition.'

On Charles de Gaulle:
'He looks like a female llama who has just been
surprised in her bath.'

On Field Marshal Lord Kitchener
(military leader and statesman; Secretary of State for War,
1914 to his death in 1916):
'He may be a general but never a gentleman.'

On Aneurin (Nye) Bevan:
'He will be as great a curse to this country in peace as he was a squalid nuisance in time of war.'

'I can think of no better step to signal the inauguration of the National Health Service than that a person who so obviously needs psychiatric attention should be among the first of its patients.'

'A merchant of discourtesy.'

'If you recognize anyone, it does not mean that you like him. We all, for instance, recognize the honourable Member for Ebbw Vale.'

Churchill did not like Aneurin Bevan and the sentiment was reciprocated. In parliamentary debates between them, Churchill usually came out on top – even if only because he could make the House laugh. One day they had a rather different confrontation. In June 1953, on the occasion of Elizabeth II's coronation, Lancaster House, newly refurbished, was the location for the Foreign Secretary's Coronation Banquet at which Churchill acted as host since Anthony Eden was ill.

After the banquet, they all repaired to Buckingham Palace where there was a State Ball. The company presented a stunning spectacle, the military and naval in full dress uniform, others decked out in fine court dress, or at the very least white tie and tails, many garlanded with decorations.

On arriving at Buckingham Palace, Churchill quickly nipped into a lavatory. When he emerged he came face to face with Bevan – wearing a blue serge suit. 'I think', admonished the Prime Minister, 'that at least on this occasion you might have taken the trouble to dress properly.'

Bevan gave a crocodile smile: 'Prime Minister, your fly buttons are undone.'

On Clement Attlee:
'A sheep in sheep's clothing.'

'If any grub is fed on Royal Jelly it turns into a Queen Bee.'

'He is a modest man who has a good deal to be modest about.'

'An empty taxi arrived at 10 Downing Street, and when the door was opened Attlee got out.'

On US President Woodrow Wilson:
'The spacious philanthropy which he exhaled upon Europe stopped quite sharply on the coasts of his own country.'

Friends like these . . .

On Lloyd George
(Liberal statesman, PM 1916–22,
and friend of Churchill):
'The Happy Warrior of Squandermania.'

On Herbert Morrison
(Labour statesman, and deputy PM in Attlee's
administration, 1945–51):
'A curious mixture of geniality and venom.'

On his friend Lord Beaverbrook
(Max Aitken, a Canadian Scot who became a Conservative MP;
and later a newspaper mogul):
'He is a foul-weather friend.'

On Hitler:
'I hate nobody except Hitler – and that is professional.'

'If Hitler invaded Hell I would make at least a favourable reference to the Devil in the House of Commons.'

On the Russian Foreign Minister Vyacheslav Mikhailovich Molotov:
'I have never seen a human being who more perfectly represented the modern concept of a robot.'

Friends like these . . .

On Stafford Cripps
(Labour statesman, Chancellor of the
Exchequer 1947–50):
'He has all the virtues I dislike and none of the vices I
admire.'

'I am glad I am not a herbivore. I eat what I like, I drink
what I like, I do what I like . . . and he's the one to have a
red nose.'

'There but for the grace of God goes God.'

'His chest is a cage in which two squirrels are at war – his
conscience and his career.'

'He delivers his speech with an expression of injured guilt.'

'a lunatic in a country of lunatics'

On T. E. Lawrence:
'He was not in complete harmony with the normal.'

'He has a way of backing into the limelight'

On Sir Dudley Pound:
'Dudley Pound's a funny old boy. People think he's always asleep, but you've only got to suggest reducing the naval estimates by a million and he's awake in a flash.'

On US Secretary of State John Foster Dulles:
'He is the only bull I know who carries his own china closet with him.'

'Dull, Duller, Dulles.'

On George Bernard Shaw:
'Few people practise what they preach and none less so than
George Bernard Shaw . . . Saint, sage and clown; venerable,
profound and irresistible.'

'He was one of my earliest antipathies. This bright, nimble,
fierce, and comprehending being – Jack Frost dancing
bespangled in the sunshine.'
Great Contemporaries

GBS: Two tickets reserved for you, first night Pygmalion.
Bring a friend. If you have one.
WSC: Cannot make first night. Will come to second.
If you have one.
An exchange of telegrams

'Of course I'm an egoist'

J ust before he started to work for Churchill, Pamela Plowden, an early love of Churchill's, told a nervous Eddie Marsh – Churchill's first Private Secretary – that 'The first time you meet Winston you see all his faults, and the rest of your life you spend in discovering his virtues.'

'Eating my words has never given me indigestion.'

'I am certainly not one of those who need to be prodded. In fact, if anything, I am a prod.'

When struck down by acute appendicitis during the 1922 election:
'I am without an office, without a seat . . . and without an appendix.'

Addressing the US Congress, December 1941:
'I cannot help reflecting that if my father had been an American and my mother British, instead of the other way round, I might have got here on my own.'

'Of course I'm an egoist'

In a discussion of standard rifles for Nato forces in 1952:
Field Marshal Sir William Slim: Well, I suppose we could experiment with a bastard rifle – partly American, partly British.
WSC: Kindly moderate your language – it may be recalled that I am myself partly British, partly American.

During a speech in Paris:
'Be on your guard! I'm going to speak in French – a formidable undertaking and one which will put great demands upon your friendship for Great Britain.'

'Everybody has the right to pronounce a foreign name as he chooses.'

Sir Cedric Hardwicke: I am honoured to learn that I am your favourite British actor.
WSC: Yesh. And my fifth favourite actor: the first four are the Marx Brothers.

'I am not usually accused even by my friends of a modest or retiring disposition.'

'I do not resent criticism, even when, for the sake of emphasis, it parts for the time with reality.'

To a woman who declared that her baby looked just like him: 'Madam, all babies look like me.'

On Churchill's eightieth birthday, in 1954, a young man was sent to take his photograph. Full of awe, he breathed, 'Sir Winston, it is wonderful to take your photograph on your eightieth birthday and I do look forward to taking it again on your hundredth birthday.' Kindly, the great man replied, 'Young man, you appear to me to be in good health and sound in wind and limb. So I see no reason why you should not.'

To his friend Leo Amery:
'I shall stick to you with all the loyalty of a leech.'

'I always manage somehow to adjust to any new level of luxury without whimper or complaint. It is one of my more winning traits.'

'If I am accused of making this mistake, I can only say with M. Clemenceau on a celebrated occasion, "Perhaps I have made a number of other mistakes of which you have not heard." '
(Georges Clemenceau led France through the First World War, and was much admired by Churchill.)

Churchill didn't tolerate fools much – or, indeed, at all – but at various times during the war was saddled with aides, usually young, who were not always as quick-witted or perceptive as they might have been. One day one of these aides, a junior officer, found Churchill reading the paper at breakfast, looking decidedly down in the mouth.

'I say, sir,' remarked the young man, 'you look rather glum.'

'I am. I've just read here' – jabbing the paper – 'that the Duke of Wellin'ton's son has been killed.'

'Oh, rotten luck! You mean the young duke, sir?'

'No! I mean the hero of the Peninshula!'

'Of course I'm an egoist'

'I have in my life concentrated more on self-expression than on self-denial.'

'I refuse to be exhibited like a prize bull whose chief attraction is his past prowess.'

On being invited by Chamberlain to meet Joachim von Ribbentrop, then German Ambassador to Britain:
'I suppose they asked me to show him that, if they couldn't bark themselves, they kept a dog who could bark and might bite.'

'It had many defects and teething troubles, and when these became apparent the tank was appropriately rechristened the "Churchill".'

'Unpunctuality is a vile habit, and all my life I have tried to break myself of it.'

'I am a sporting man. I always like to give trains and aeroplanes a fair chance of getting away.'

'I suppress with difficulty an impulse to become sententious.'

'All the years that I have been in the House of Commons I have always said to myself one thing:
"Do not interrupt" and I have never been able to keep to that resolution.'

Childlike, Churchill believed that wherever he was his domestic routine would be the same as at home. One day, when the Supreme War Council were meeting at the Château du Muguet in June 1940 – just after Dunkirk, with the fall of France imminent – General Spears reported, two French officers, drinking coffee in the dining room, were alarmed by the doors being flung open and 'an apparition which they said resembled an angry Japanese genie, in long, flowing red silk kimono over other similar but white garments, girdled with a white belt' burst in, 'sparse hair on end' and loudly demanded, 'Oo ay ma ban?'

'I am always ready to learn although I do not always like being taught.'

On his seventy-fifth birthday:
'I am ready to meet my Maker. Whether my Maker is ready for the ordeal of meeting me is another matter.'

'Of course I'm an egoist. Where do you get if you aren't?'

Sir Samuel Hoare: 'Winston has written a huge book all about himself and called it *The World Crisis*.'
WSC: 'I have not always been wrong. History will bear me out, particularly as I shall write that history myself.'

'Although always prepared for martyrdom, I preferred that it should be postponed.'
My Early Life

To his daughter Sarah:
'Do you know what happened to me today? The Turkish President kissed me. The truth is I'm irresistible. But don't tell Anthony – he's jealous.'
(Eden was Foreign Secretary at the time; he was to succeed Churchill as Prime Minister in 1955.)

'The world is not made up of heroes and heroines – luckily
or where would you and I find our backgrounds!'
Letter to Margot Asquith

*On attending a dinner for the Prince of Wales,
later Edward VII, in 1896*:
'I realized that I must be on my best behaviour – punctual,
subdued, reserved – in short, display all the qualities with
which I am the least endowed.'

'I wonder what God thinks of the things His creatures have
invented. Really, it's surprising He has allowed it – but then
I suppose He has so many things to think of, not only us,
but all His worlds. I wouldn't have his job for anything.
Mine is hard enough, but His is much more difficult. And –
umph – He can't even resign . . .'

'My idea of a good dinner is, first to have good food, then discuss good food, and after this good food has been elaborately discussed, to discuss a good topic – with me as chief conversationalist.'

On death and the afterlife:
'Some kind of velvety cool blackness. Of course, I admit I may be wrong. It is conceivable that I might well be reborn as a Chinese coolie. In such a case I should lodge a protest.'

'Everyone will have equal rights in Heaven. That will be the real Welfare State . . .'

'Megalomania is the only form of sanity.'

'What kind of people?': The Nations according to Churchill

On one occasion when he was Prime Minister, Churchill had a brief meeting with his counterpart in the Republic of Ireland at a time when both countries were facing serious problems. When Churchill remarked to the Irish PM that, in his view, the situation in the United Kingdom was serious but not hopeless, the Irish Prime Minister replied – according to Churchill – that the situation in his country was hopeless but not serious. But, while he often found amusement in other nations, he never failed to see the idiosyncrasies of his own.   Likewise, Churchill's attitude towards speaking foreign languages was idiosyncratic. Complaining, in 1940, of the lack of unity in the French government and the precious time this was wasting, he baffled a French guest by announcing, 'Nous allons perdre l'omnibus.'

'The English never draw a line without blurring it.'

'Frightfulness is not a remedy known to the British pharmacopoeia.'

'There are few virtues that the Poles do not possess – and there are few errors they have ever avoided.'

On America:
'Toilet paper too thin, newspapers too fat.'

On Russia:
'Here we have a state whose subjects are so happy that they have to be forbidden to quit its bounds under the direst penalties; whose diplomatists and agents sent on foreign missions have often to leave their wives and children at home to ensure their eventual return.'

'Everybody has always underrated the Russians. They keep their own secrets alike from foe and friends.'

'Premier Stalin, whose conduct of foreign policy manifests a desire for peace.'
[*then, in a whispered aside*] 'A piece of Poland, a piece of Czechoslovakia, a piece of Romania . . .'

'In Russia a man is called reactionary if he objects to having his property stolen and his wife and children murdered.'

A few years before the outbreak of the First World War, Churchill was at a diplomatic reception. An Italian military attaché asked a Luxembourgeois diplomat about a medal he was wearing. 'It is an ancient order called the Royal Admiralty Cross,' the diplomat replied stiffly. After he had stalked off, the Italian turned to the First Lord of the Admiralty, Winston Churchill, and remarked how odd it was that Luxembourg should have this when it did not even have a navy. 'Why shouldn't they have an admiralty?' Churchill answered cheerfully. 'You in Italy, after all, have a minister of finance – yet you don't have a treasury!'

'The Almighty in His infinite wisdom did not see fit to create Frenchmen in the image of Englishmen.'

To his French translator:
'Until I heard your splendid version, Monsieur, I did not realize what a magnificent, indeed epoch-making, speech I had made. Allow me to embrace you, Monsieur.'

Securing the wholehearted compliance of the Free French during the war was not always easy, especially when it required the co-operation of both de Gaulle and the Vichy French. Urged by a diplomat to coddle de Gaulle's pride with flattery, Churchill is said to have to have agreed: 'I'll kiss him on both cheeks – or, if you prefer, on all four.'

To de Gaulle:
'Si vous m'obstaclerez, je vous liquiderai.'

'For good or for ill the French people have been effective masters in their own house, and have built as they chose upon the ruins of the old regime. Their difficulty is to like what they have done.'

Jock Colville recalled an instance in 1941 when as Churchill's Private Secretary he was caught uncomfortably between Churchill and de Gaulle. General de Gaulle was at the time being a less than helpful ally and the Prime Minister, considerably annoyed by his behaviour, summoned him to Downing Street. He informed Jock Colville that he would not shake hands with de Gaulle and would not speak with him in French but through an interpreter – and that Colville himself was to be the interpreter.

The General arrived at the due time and was ushered into the Cabinet Room. True to his word, Churchill did not shake his hand, merely indicating a seat across the table from himself. 'General de Gaulle, I have asked you to come here this afternoon,' he started and looked fiercely at Colville, who translated: 'Mon Général, je vous ai invité . . .'

'I *didn't* say "Mon Général",' objected Churchill petulantly, 'and I did not say I had *invited* him.'

Colville struggled on for a few sentences, with many interruptions from his boss. Then de Gaulle spoke and Colville interpreted – to be interrupted by, 'Non, non. Ce n'est pas du tout le sens de ce que je disais.' At which Churchill said that if he could not do any better he had better find someone who could. Colville escaped and summoned someone from the Foreign Office whose French was impeccable. The official arrived and Colville showed him into the Cabinet Room (in which not a word had been spoken during the interval).

Within minutes the man from the Foreign Office came out

red-faced, and spluttering that they had to be mad: they had said he could not speak French properly and they would have to manage without an interpreter.

The soundproof double doors of the Cabinet Room were closed and nothing could be heard. Over an hour passed and Colville was beginning to get anxious – 'Perhaps they had strangled each other?' But then the bell rang and he went in – to find the two men sitting amicably side by side, smoking cigars and chatting – in French.

On the Japanese:
'It becomes still more difficult to reconcile Japanese action with prudence or even sanity. What kind of people do they think we are?'

'The Japanese, whose game is what I may call to make hell while the sun shines . . .'

When staying at the White House as a guest of President Roosevelt, Churchill naturally had a bathroom to himself and could have a bath whenever he wished. Roosevelt's son recalled his father trundling into Churchill's room in his wheelchair to see his guest, and being startled to catch a naked Churchill just stepping out of his bath. He hurriedly set about reversing his wheelchair but was stopped by Churchill: 'The Prime Minister has nothing to hide from the President of the United States.'

In 1943 Churchill sent Anthony Eden on a mission to bring Turkey into the war.
Eden: Progress slow. What more can I tell Turkey?
WSC: Tell them Christmas is coming!

'India is a geographical term. It is no more a united nation than the Equator.'

Henpecked?:
Women and the
Family

Churchill was probably typical of his time in his attitude towards the family, women, and women's rights. He had been brought up to believe that the women ran the household, tended the husband and bore and looked after children. Family life and motherhood, he once claimed, 'must be the fountain spring of present happiness and future survival'. His pronouncement 'You must have four children. One for Mother, one for Father, one for Accidents, one for Increase' has a very Victorian ring to it – although it could have been uttered tongue-in-cheek. Women were not inferior beings but they were different beings, and he could not see the point of giving women the vote – their husbands or fathers handled that side of life for them. He at first found the idea of women's suffrage hard to accept – being particularly put off by violent demonstrations – and just as he was coming round to the idea – 'I am anxious to see women relieved in principle from a disability which is injurious to them,' he wrote – he was almost pushed under a train by an angry suffragette in 1909 and had to be rescued by his wife. It was not until 1918 that women got the vote (those over thirty, the age lowered to twenty-one ten years later). He would probably have said that, at home, his wife Clementine ruled supreme – most of the time.

Other women in his life included his secretaries. He worked

them hard – to the point of making them stay up all night taking dictation – ('I shall need two women tonight' he would say to his Private Secretary at busy times, no doubt loudly enough to startle any guest not in the know); and he was kind to them, if sometimes irritable and impatient. Almost without exception they, and also his male research assistants and Private Secretaries, grew to love him – 'His secretaries adored him . . . We were all in love with him; he was such a lovely man,' said Maurice Ashley, one of his research assistants.

'You must have four children. One for Mother, one for Father, one for Accidents, one for Increase.'

'Nothing would induce me to vote for giving women the franchise. I am not going to be henpecked into a question of such importance.'

'At Blenheim I took two very important decisions: to be born and to marry. I am content with the decision I took on both occasions.'

'I married and lived happily ever after'
My Early Life

'It's an extraordinary business, this way of bringing babies into the world. I don't know how God thought if it.'

'My wife and I tried two or three times in the last few years to have breakfast together but it was so disagreeable we had to stop.'

At a reception in Richmond, Virginia, in the USA, Churchill's hostess, an ample lady, led the guest of honour, to the buffet table. When she offered him some cold chicken, he asked if he could have a breast. As she helped him to a particularly succulent-looking piece his hostess informed him genteelly that 'We Southern ladies use the term "white meat".'

The next day a corsage arrived for her – with the flowers was a card from Churchill on which he had written 'I would be most obliged if you would pin this on your "white meat".'

While in Washington during a speaking tour of the States, in 1900, Churchill was introduced to a generously proportioned woman – from Richmond, Virginia. Proud of her family's adherence to the former Confederacy, and still not accepting the Reconstruction – the process of incorporating the Southern states into the United States – she declared, as she gave him her hand, 'Mr Churchill, you see before you a rebel who has not been Reconstructed.'

'Madam,' he replied, gazing upon her imposing bosom, 'reconstruction in your case would be blasphemous.'

At the unveiling of a sculpture of WSC in Richmond, Virginia, a magnificently Rubenesque lady came up to him and cooed enthusiastically: 'Mr Churchill, I want you to know I got up at dawn and drove a hundred miles for the unveiling of your bust.'

Looking upon her generous endowments, WSC answered, 'Madam, I want you to know that I would happily reciprocate the honour.'

At a reception in Canada WSC happened to be seated next to a very strait-laced Methodist minister, when a pert young waitress came up to them with a tray of glasses of sherry. She went first to Churchill, who took a glass, and then turned to the minister. He was appalled to be offered alcohol: 'Young lady,' he announced, 'I'd rather commit adultery than take an intoxicating beverage.' Whereupon Churchill beckoned the girl: 'Come back, miss – I didn't know we had a choice.'

On Nancy Astor:
'She enjoys the best of both worlds . . . she denounces the vice of gambling in unmeasured terms, and is closely associated with an almost unrivalled racing stable. She accepts Communist hospitality and flattery, and remains the Conservative Member for Plymouth.'
Great Contemporaries

'It must be a great pleasure for the noble lady, the member for the Sutton Division of Plymouth, to see me drink water.'

'Nancy, when you entered the House, I felt you had come upon me in my bath and I had nothing to protect me but my sponge.'

Nancy Astor: 'If I were your wife I would put poison in your coffee.'

Churchill: 'Nancy, if I were your husband, I would drink it.'

Woman: 'There are two things I don't like about you, Mr Churchill – your politics and your moustache.'

WSC: 'My dear madam, pray do not disturb yourself. You are not likely to come into contact with either.'

Bessie Braddock: 'Winston, you're drunk.'

WSC: 'Madam, you're ugly. But tomorrow I shall be shober.'

'It is hard, if not impossible, to snub a beautiful woman – they remain beautiful and the rebuke recoils.'

Question: If you could not be who you are,
who would you like to be?
WSC's answer: Mrs Churchill's second husband.

'My most brilliant achievement was to persuade my wife
to marry me.'

Vic Oliver (*WSC's son-in-law*): Who, in your opinion, is
the greatest statesman you know?
WSC: Benito Mussolini.
Oliver: What? Why?
WSC: Mussolini is the only statesman who had the requisite
courage to have his son-in-law executed.

WSC's grandson: Grandpapa! Are you really the greatest
man in the world?
WSC: Of course I am the greatest man in the world.
Now bu– buzz off.

Henpecked?

On the actions of the suffragettes:
'I might as well chain myself to St Thomas's [Hospital] and say I would not move until I had had a baby!'

'An ineradicable
habit':
Drink

Whether or not Churchill had a 'drink problem' seems to have been for long a favourite topic for discussion. That he enjoyed alcohol – especially whisky, brandy and champagne – is beyond doubt, but that he was a drunkard seems quite unlikely. His slight speech impediment, slurring S's into Shs and Zhs, might have suggested to those who did not know any better the speech of a drinker – and it could well have suited Churchill from time to time to give the impression that he was the worse for drink, that his brain was perhaps not working as acutely as it actually was . . . In general, the alcohol issue fed his sense of mischief: while he had a proper respect for fine brandies or champagnes, it amused him to talk about his drinking habits, and to tease teetotallers. (And apparently after Churchill's car accident in January 1932 in New York, Dr Otto C. Pickhardt wrote a prescription for him . . . 'the use of alcoholic spirits at meal times . . . the minimum requirement to be 250 cc'.) Drunkenness, on the other hand, was not on: 'I have been brought up and trained to have the utmost contempt for people who get drunk,' he wrote in *My Early Life*.

Field Marshal Montgomery: I neither drink nor smoke and am a hundred per cent fit.
WSC: I drink and smoke and am two hundred per cent fit.

'When I was a young subaltern in the South African War, the water was not fit to drink. To make it palatable we had to add whisky. By diligent effort I learned to like it.'

'I neither want it [brandy] nor need it, but I should think it pretty hazardous to interfere with the ineradicable habit of a lifetime.'

In a letter to his wife on having moved, ahead of her, into Chartwell:
'I drink champagne at all meals & buckets of claret & soda in between . . .'

One of Churchill's frequent visitors in the years before the war was Major Desmond Morton, a former member of the government's secret Industrial Intelligence Centre. When, after the war, Jock Colville asked Churchill outright if Morton had been giving him more information than the government would have approved, Churchill's answer was, 'Have another drop of brandy.'

'I must point out that my rule of life prescribes as an absolutely sacred rite smoking cigars and also the drinking of alcohol before, after, and if need be during all meals and in the intervals between them.'

'No one can say that I ever failed to display a meet and proper appreciation of alcohol.'

'Always remember, Clemmie, that I have taken more out of alcohol than alcohol has taken out of me.'

'When I was younger I made it a rule never to take strong drink before lunch. It is now my rule never to do so before breakfast.'

'A single glass of champagne imparts a feeling of exhilaration. The nerves are braced, the imagination is agreeably stirred, the wits become more nimble. A bottle produces the contrary effect.'

It is related that when Churchill was First Lord of the Admiralty, he was approached by a temperance group suggesting that he should reconsider the maritime tradition of christening a ship by breaking a bottle of champagne across the bow.

'But, madam,' Churchill replied to the spokeswoman, 'the hallowed custom of the Royal Navy is indeed a splendid example of temperance. The ship takes its first sip of wine and then proceeds on water ever after.'

'Good cognac is like a woman. Do not assault it. Coddle
and warm it in your hands before you sip it.'

When many of the trees at Chartwell were lost in
the 1987 'hurricane' a large number of them were
replaced by the Pol Roger family. It is said, too, that during
the Second World War, Madame Pol Roger had two cases of
champagne for Churchill, which she kept hidden from the
Nazis. Needless to say, Pol Roger champagne was Churchill's
favourite.

'Our maxims will remain': Epigrams

Like all self-respecting wits, Churchill was a fount of epigrams – his own, 'borrowed' ones, and well-known ones that he adapted.

Among his most famous words is the epigraph:

> In war: resolution
> In defeat: defiance
> In victory: magnanimity
> In peace: goodwill.

(It is said to have originally been offered, at the end of the First World War, to a French town as a memorial; the lines, however, were politely declined – apparently on the grounds that the shattered citizens found the idea of magnanimity and goodwill too hard to take. Certainly French 'reparations' against Germany at Versailles bear this out.)

'Too often the strong silent man is silent because he does not know what to say, and is reputed strong only because he has remained silent.'

'It is better to be making the news than taking it; to be an actor rather than a critic.'

'Perhaps it is better to be irresponsible and right than to be responsible and wrong.'

'A fanatic is one who can't change his mind and won't change the subject.'

'It is a fine thing to be honest, but it is also very important to be right.'

‘Our maxims will remain’

‘Art is to beauty what honour is to honesty.’

‘Without tradition art is a flock of sheep without a shepherd. Without innovation it is a corpse.’

‘Youth is for freedom and reform, maturity for judicious compromise, and old age for stability and repose.’

‘Civil servants – no longer servants, no longer civil.’

‘If the present tries to sit in judgement of the past, it will lose the future.’

'When civilization degenerates our morals will be gone but our maxims will remain.'

'Diplomacy is the art of telling plain truths without giving offence.'

'Everyone has his day and some days last longer than others.'

'Do not let the better be the enemy of the good.'

'There are a terrible lot of lies going around the world, and the worst of it is half of them are true.'

'We are happier in many ways when we are old than when we are young. The young sow wild oats, the old grow sage.'

'War is mainly a catalogue of blunders.'

'A nation that forgets its past has no future.'

'Never stand so high upon a principle that you cannot lower it to suit the circumstances.'

'It is always wise to look ahead, but difficult to look farther than you can see.'

'You will never get to the end of the journey if you stop to shy a stone at every dog that barks.'

'Virtuous motives, trammelled by inertia and timidity, are no match for armed and resolute wickedness.'

'The worst quarrels only arise when both sides are equally in the right and in the wrong.'

'Criticism is easy; achievement is difficult.'

'It is always more easy to discover and proclaim general principles than to apply them.'

'Never trust a man who has not a single redeeming vice.'

'It is wonderful how well men can keep secrets they have not been told.'

'Sometimes truth is so precious, it must be attended by a bodyguard of lies.'

'Difficulties mastered are opportunities won.'

Miscellanea

Churchill never failed to find opportunity for wit in almost any situation, whether on the golf course, during a tour of duty, or when with his family, having withdrawn from public life. During the last years of his life he spent his time quietly – sometimes in France, sometimes at Chartwell – where he would enjoy visits from friends, with whom he played cards, or talked at length. At times he lamented that he was no longer capable of original thought – but would sometimes surprise himself by coming out with some sharp and shrewd comment. Even at the very end of his life, when it sometimes appeared that he was lost in a world of his own he would join in the conversation with a sudden and relevant remark. 'I decline utterly to be impartial as between the fire brigade and the fire.' (Speaking to the House in July 1926, during the General Strike, Churchill was responding to complaints about bias in his editing of the *British Gazette*.)

'Physician, comb thyself.'
(The 'physician' in this speech to the House of Commons in May 1916 was the War Office, which was calling for the 'combing-out', or pruning, of industries and of other government departments.)

In the early days of the Blitz, Churchill was driven to Canterbury where he went to view the cathedral being bolstered with sandbags. The Archbishop was gloomy, and the Prime Minister attempted to bolster him up too: 'No matter how many close hits the Nazis may make, I feel sure the cathedral will survive.' 'Ah, *close* hits . . . ,' said the Archbishop glumly. 'But what if we get a *direct* hit?'

'In that event,' the Prime Minister responded, losing patience, 'you will have to regard it, my dear Archbishop, as a divine summons.'

When Clementine remarked that his defeat in 1945 was perhaps a blessing in disguise:
'If it is a blessing, it is certainly very well disguised.'

On being asked if the Niagara Falls looked the same as when he first saw them:
'Well, the principle seems the same. The water still keeps falling over.'

Travelling across the United States in 1929, with his son Randolph, brother Jack and Jack's boy, Johnny, Churchill's itinerary took in Hollywood, where he met Charlie Chaplin. In conversation with him, Churchill asked what film part he would like to do next. In all seriousness, Chaplin replied, 'I'd like to play Jesus Christ.'

Without batting an eyelid, WSC asked him: 'Have you cleared the rights?'

To Roosevelt on the Normandy beachhead on D-Day-plus-6 (12 June 1944):
'Wish you were here.'

A famous early indication of Churchill's defiant nature occurred at Harrow when, aged thirteen or so, he was summoned before the headmaster over some matter of ill-discipline or idleness. 'I have very grave reason to be displeased with you,' intoned the good Mr Welldon (for whom Churchill long retained an affection). 'And I, sir, have very grave reason to be displeased with you,' rejoined the boy.

On another occasion at school, Churchill was asked by his Latin teacher to decline *mensa* (table). The boy proceeded to do so, giving the nominative, accusative, genitive, dative and ablative. 'The vocative?' prompted his teacher.

'But I don't intend ever to talk to tables,' Churchill replied reasonably, if impertinently.

To Roosevelt in 1942:
'It's a nuizenza to have the fluenza.'

When asked what he thought of American football:
'Actually it is somewhat like rugby. But why do you have all these committee meetings?'

*To Roosevelt on establishing the UN during the six days
of the Yalta conference:*
'I don't see any way of realizing our hopes for a World
Organization in six days. Even the Almighty took seven.'

BBC spokesman on a forthcoming programme entitled
Christianity vs. Atheism: It is our duty to truth to allow
both sides to debate.
WSC: I suppose, then, that if there had been the same
devices at the time of Christ the BBC would have given
equal time to Judas and Jesus.

'Golf is like chasing a quinine pill around a pasture.'

'Golf is a game whose aim is to hit a very small ball into an
even smaller hole, with weapons singularly ill designed for
the purpose.'

Dismayed at the comparative failure of the United Kingdom to produce as many scientists and engineers as the United States, Churchill spoke soon after ending his last term as Prime Minister about how he should have tried to see the establishment in Britain of an equivalent to the Massachusetts Institute of Technology. His former secretary Jock Colville and others immediately set about making amends, raising funds for a new college which was to be part of Cambridge University and devoted to science and technology. It was suggested that the new college be named after Churchill. When Colville relayed this suggestion to Churchill, his reaction was not one of immediate gratification – to have a memorial in his own lifetime, and in a university when, despite his many honorary degrees and Chancellorship of Bristol University, he had never gone to university, must have seemed strange. But Colville persisted: 'What memorial could be more lasting than a great university college?'

After a pause, WSC replied: 'It is very nice of them. And I ought certainly to be pleased. After all, it will put me alongside the Trinity.'

While visiting a parachute factory, Churchill absentmindedly took out a cigar.
Fire officer: Sir, sir, you mustn't smoke!
WSC: Oh, don't worry, dear boy. I don't inhale.

*When seated with the director-general of the BBC, Lord Reith, a
tall Presbyterian Scot of gloomy aspect*:
'Who will rescue me from this Wuthering Height?'

'Scientists should be on tap but not on top.'

'I have always considered that the substitution of the
internal combustion engine for the horse marked a very
gloomy milestone for the progress of mankind.'

'There ought to be a hagiology of medical
science and we ought to have saints' days to
commemorate the great discoveries which have
been made for all mankind . . . a holiday, a day
of jubilation when we can fête St Anaesthesia,
and pure and chaste St Antiseptic . . . and if I
had a vote I should be bound to celebrate
St Penicillin.'

'The latest refinements of science are linked with the cruelties of the Stone Age.'

On contracting a staphylococcus infection in June 1946:
'The bug seems to have caught my truculence. This is its finest hour.'

'Where there is a great deal of free speech, there is always a certain amount of foolish speech.'

'Everyone is in favour of free speech. Hardly a day passes without its being extolled, but some people's idea of it is that they are free to say what they like, but if anyone says anything back, that is an outrage.'

'When you have to kill a man it costs nothing to be polite.'

'Mr Gladstone read Homer for fun, which I thought
served him right.'

'There is a rule that before getting a new book, one
should read an old classic. Yet, as an author, I should not
recommend too strict an adherence to this rule.'

'We have never been likely to get into trouble by having
an extra thousand or two of up-to-date aeroplanes at our
disposal . . . As the man whose mother-in-law had died
in Brazil replied, when asked how the remains should be
disposed of: "Embalm, cremate, and bury. Take no risks!" '

Following the British withdrawal in 1940 from Norway, it was proposed that the Royal Marines should all have sheaths to protect the exposed muzzles of their rifles from the sharp temperature changes for their next foray into Norway. A pharmaceutical company that specialized in manufacturing condoms was given the job. In due course the first box was delivered for the Prime Minister's inspection. He looked at the box and muttered, 'Won't do.' He drew a carton out of the box, shook his head and muttered 'Won't do' again. He opened the carton and took out a packet. 'Won't do,' he reiterated.

'What do you mean it won't do?' an aide asked him. 'They are long enough for the muzzles – ten and a half inches.'

'Labels,' came the cryptic reply.

'*Labels?*'

'Yes. I want a label for every box, every carton, every packet, saying "British. Size: Medium". That will show the Nazis, if they ever recover one of them, who's the master race.'

When asked by Lord Londonderry if he had read his last book:
'No, I only read for pleasure or for profit.'

On painting:
'I prefer landscapes. A tree doesn't complain
that I haven't done it justice.'

'I cannot pretend to feel impartial about
colours. I rejoice with the brilliant ones and am
genuinely sorry for the poor browns.'

'There are men in the world who derive as stern an
exaltation from the proximity of disaster and ruin, as others
from success.'

Referring to Rudolph Hess's parachute descent into Scotland:
'This is one of those cases in which the imagination is
baffled by the facts.'

Sitting in the House of Commons in 1956, listening to Hugh Gaitskell speaking on economic issues, Churchill suddenly began rummaging through his pockets, and then bending down to search the floor and under his seat. Gaitskell, completely thrown off-track, stopped speaking and asked if he could help. 'I was only looking for my jujube,' WSC answered in a small voice, loud enough to be heard by the whole House. (The following day the newspapers wrote this up under the heading 'the Fall of the Pastille'.)

'Of this I am quite sure, that if we open a quarrel between the past and the present, we shall find we have lost the future.'

On the mistakes made in the First World War:
'I am sure that the mistakes of that time will not be repeated; we should probably make another set of mistakes.'